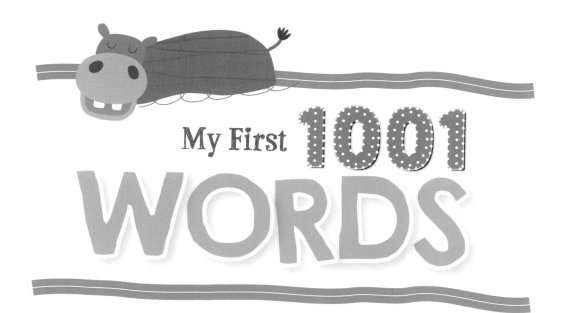

My First 1001 WORDS

This book belongs to:

· ·

· ·

HOW THE APP WORKS

This book comes with a free app that allows you to use your smartphone or tablet to hear the pronunciation of over 1000 words and short sentences!

1. DOWNLOAD THE APP from the App Store (if you have an iOS device) or from Google Play (if your tablet or smartphone runs on Android). Type in "MyFirst1001Words" and look for the puppy icon shown here. The information pages on each app store will tell you what operating system and device you will need to run the app. Click on the icon to download the app onto your smartphone or tablet.

2. LAUNCH the app. You will be asked to authorise access to your camera. The app works best in strong light and with flattened pages. Hover with your smartphone or tablet at least a foot above the pages (from 6 to 59). White loudspeaker icons will pop up on your screen.

3. TAP ON THE ICONS TO HEAR the words pronounced by a native speaker. You can tap as many times as you like. Don't forget to adjust the volume on your device. The app contains British English pronunciation.

First published in Great Britain in 2021 by NQ Publishers, an imprint of Nextquisite Ltd.

Copyright © 2020 by Nextquisite Ltd

Project Director Anne McRae; Art Director: Marco Nardi
Text: Elizabeth Cranford; Illustrations: Craig Shuttlewood
ISBN 978-1-912944-71-2
Printed in China

DISCLAIMER
This app runs on (**iOS** 11 or later) *iPhone* SE, 6s, 6s Plus, 7, 7 Plus, 8, X; all *iPad Pro* models and *iPad* (2017 onwards). For **Android** (7 or later) you can find a complete list of compatible devices by scanning the QR code on the panda or by visiting https://developers.google.com/ar/discover/supported-devices#google_play

My First 1001 WORDS

Illustrated by Craig Shuttlewood

from Aardvark to Zero

and all the words in between

NQ
PUBLISHERS

For enquiring minds

FINDING TOBY
Our dog Toby has hidden himself on every page. Can you spot him?

4

TABLE OF CONTENTS

5

THIS IS ME

How big are you? Can you wash your face? Can you brush your teeth? What colour is your hair? Is it short or long?

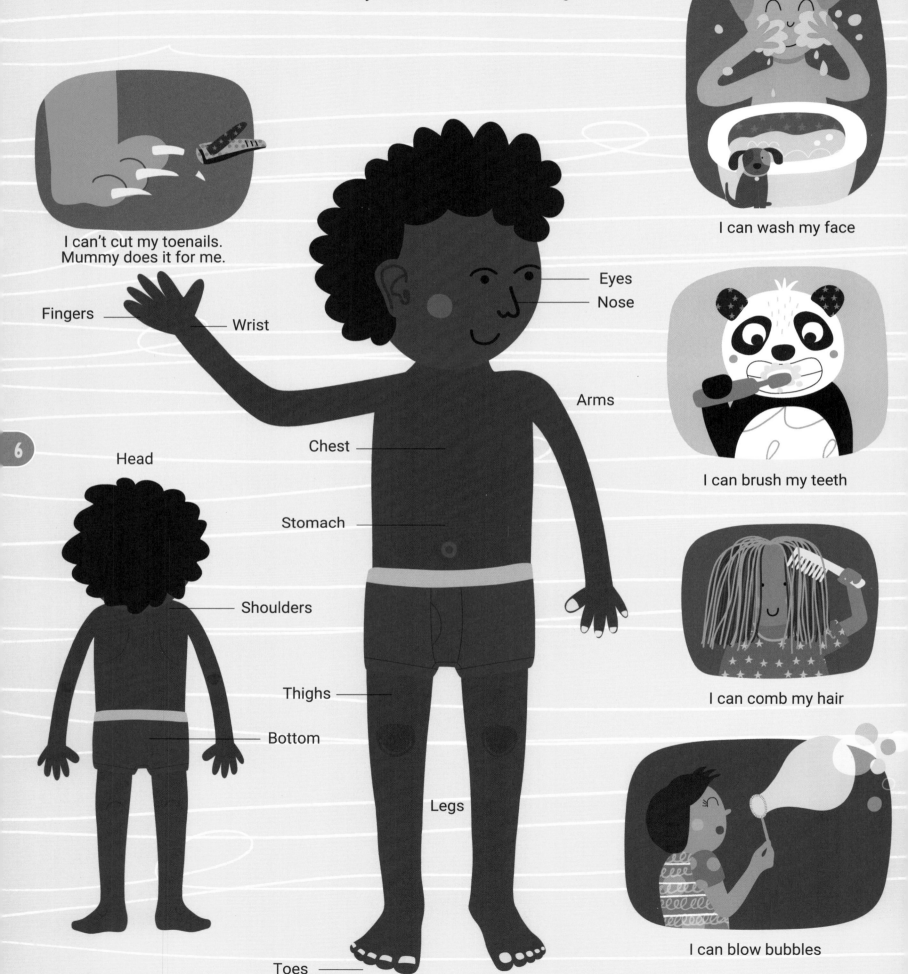

I can't cut my toenails. Mummy does it for me.

Fingers

Wrist

Head

Shoulders

Thighs

Bottom

Eyes

Nose

Arms

Chest

Stomach

Legs

Toes

I can wash my face

I can brush my teeth

I can comb my hair

I can blow bubbles

6

Ponytail

Hair

I can smell the flowers

Ears

Face

Cheeks

Mouth

Chin

I can taste the carrot

I can feel the teddy

Neck

Back

Thumb

I can see the dove

Hand

Knees

Ankles

Feet

I can hear the music

7

Vest

Dress

Jeans

Shirt

Pyjamas

Socks

Pants

T-shirt

Shorts

Swimming trunks

Swimsuit

Shoes

Wellies

Sandals

Trainers

Slippers

Shelf

WHAT SHALL I WEAR?

Look at all the clothes hanging on the lines.
See the shoes and bags on the shelf.
Are you wearing any of these things?

Floats

What do you wear
to go swimming?

What do you
wear to school?

Shirt

Shorts

Skirt

What do you
wear to bed?

Jacket

Dressing gown

Trousers

Sweater

Coat

Hat

Tights

Skirt

Bib

Onsie

Heels

Handbag

Gloves

Rucksack

Belt

9

DRESSING-UP CLOTHES

What can you see in the dressing-up box?
Can you see...
A crown?
A wand?
A mask?
A necklace?
Some sunglasses?

What do you wear to a party?

A party hat!

Fairy wings

Hat

Mask

Crown

Cap

Ring

Tiara

Boots

Sunglasses

Necklace

MY FAMILY

Here is my family. There are quite a few of us!
I'm not really married, but I may be one day.
When I grow up I may have children and
grandchildren.

GRANDPARENTS

Grandfather

Grandmother

PARENTS

Mother

Father

Boyfriend   Girlfriend

Sister-in-law

Brother

Sister

ME

Niece

Nephew

Son

Husband   Wife

Wedding

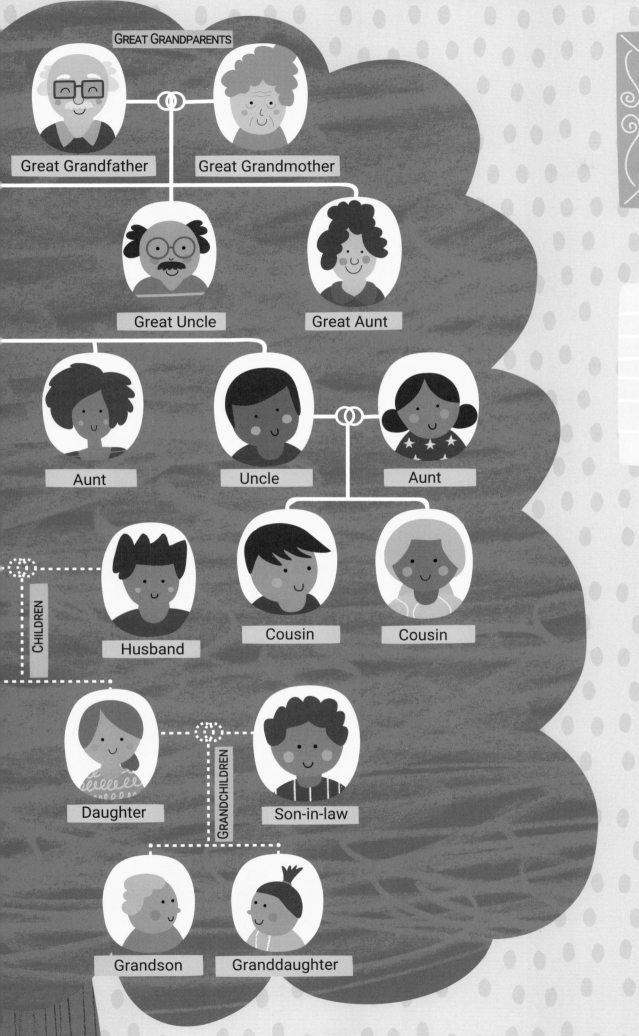

GREAT GRANDPARENTS

Great Grandfather

Great Grandmother

Great Uncle

Great Aunt

Aunt

Uncle

Aunt

CHILDREN

Husband

Cousin

Cousin

Daughter

GRANDCHILDREN

Son-in-law

Grandson

Granddaughter

Twins

Triplets

11

Baby

AT HOME

Here you can see a house and garden. How many rooms can you see in the house? Who is popping his head out of the garden shed? Is it a goat?

Tree

Tree house

Flower

Skylark

Garden shed

Rose

Fence

Flower bed

Rose bush

Watering can

Wheelbarrow

Spade

13

Garden hose

Carrots

Shrub

Lawnmower

Broccoli

Beets

Lawn

Lettuces

Cabbages

Slug

Worm

Vegetable patch

Blind

Herbs

Glass

Teapot

Washing up liquid

Tap

Bread

Sharp knife

Sponges

Toaster

Kettle

Sink

Chopping board

Cupboards

Dishwasher

14

Rubbish bin

Chair

IN THE KITCHEN

The kitchen is the room where you cook food. If you have a big table you can also eat in the kitchen. If you spill some food on the floor, what would you use to mop it up?

Kitchen table

Mug

Bowl

FOOD

What do you eat for breakfast? Do you have toast and jam or cereal with milk? Are strawberries your favourite fruit?

Breakfast

Coffee

Jam

Toast

Croissant

Milk

Butter

Tea

Bacon

Leeks

Cereal

Courgettes (Zucchini)

Eggs

Salad

Lunch

Peas

celery

Radish

Carrot

Omelette

Tomatoes

Mushrooms

16

Oranges

Limes

Lemons

Asparagus

Strawberries

Cheese

Pasta

Sausages

Figs

Sausage rolls

Corn

Dinner

Rice

Watermelon

Pineapple

Potatoes

Chicken

Peppers

Biscuits (cookies)

Cake

Muffin

Pie

Cupcakes

Blueberries

17

LIVING ROOM

Picture

Curtains

Digital clock

15:25

Vase

Mantlepiece

Window

Sideboard

Fireplace

Television

Pot plant

Armchair

Remote

Bug

Sofa

Carpet

Cushion

Lamp

Coffee table

18

BATHROOM

Mirror

Towel rack

Toilet

Shower

Wash basin

Shelf

Toothbrush

Towel

Toothpaste

Rubber duck

Comb

Tiles

Bathtub

MY ROOM

Poster

Llama

19

Chest of drawers

Radiator

Wardrobe

Toy box

Floor

Pillow

Toys

Bed

Rug

Duvet

Bedside table

AT SCHOOL

Going to school is fun. You can draw pictures, write stories and play with your friends. Do you like going to school? Can you read?

Principal (Headmaster)

Laptop

Writing

Desk

Pencil

Teacher's desk

20

Recorder

Reading

Drum

Pupil

Music

Story book

Mat

Chalk

Whiteboard

Class 4B

Clock

Globe

Books

Map

Bookcase

Backpack

Teacher

Chair

Paper

Computer

Science

Letters - Alphabet

A B C D E F G
H I J K L M
N O P Q R S T
U V W X Y Z

Screen

Keyboard

Brushes

Glue

Drawing

Rubber

Crayons

Painting

2+2=
1+3=
3+6=

10+1=
8+4=
8+2=

History

Maths

21

IN THE CITY

It is busy in the city. Where would you go to buy a book? Where would you go to buy some food? Where could you see a movie?

Museum

Car park

Mosque

Hospital

Skyscrapers

River

Fish

Doctor's surgery

Doctor

Seagull

22

Ambulance

School

Church

Bicycle

Greengrocer

Bookshop

Café

TAXI

Hairdresser

Boutique

Butcher

Taxi

Veterinary surgery

Supermarket

Police station

Temple

Dentist

Cinema

Synagogue

Library

Fountain

Bus stop

Block of flats

23

Street

Bus

Town Hall

House

House

Fire Station

Statue

Underground

Baker

Restaurant

Bank

Theatre

Car

AT THE PARK

There is plenty to do at the park. You can row on the lake or play on the swings. You can bring food and have a picnic or barbecue. What do you like to do at the park?

Running track

Helmet

Deck chairs

Cyclist

Jogger

Duck

24

Lily

Pedalo

Drinking fountain

Fish

Rowing boat

2

Frog

Lake

Flowers

Path

Picnic table

Cake

Who is having a picnic?

Hot dog

Picnic

Barbecue

Picnic blanket

Kite

Squirrels

Tennis court

Public toilets

Litter bin

Climbing frame

Dog walker

25

Playhouse

Park bench

Skipping rope

Basketball hoop

Swing

Sandpit

Slide

Playground

Roundabout

Seesaw

Sprinkler

AT THE BEACH

It is a hot summer day and we are at the beach. Some people are swimming or playing in the sea, while others are sleeping in the sun. Can you spot the amazing surfing sheep?

Sea

Surf

Waves

Surfing sheep

Jet ski

Seagull

Crab

Snorkel

Sunglasses

Scuba diver

Life preserver

Fish

Surfboard

Trunks

Seashells

Crab

Swimsuit

Flip flops

Starfish

Mussel

Rock

Flippers

26

Seagull

Beach ball

Inflatable air mattress

Palm trees

Boat

Lilo

Refreshment stand

Swimming

ICE CREAM VAN

Ice creams

27

Sand

Sandcastle

Sunhat

Sun umbrella

Pail

Spade

Beach towels

Cooler

Beach chair

Sunscreen

ON THE FARM

Look at all the animals on the farm. Dogs go "bow wow" and cows go "moo". How many animal noises can you make? Can you name all the baby animals?

Hen house

Farmhouse

Wheelbarrow

Rooster

Hen

Chicken

Farm truck

Farmer

Bucket

Turkey

Fence

28

Pond

Cat

Kitten

Sheepdog

Puppy

Goose

Bees

Duckling

Who is swimming in the pond?

Gosling

Beehives

Ducks

Bat

Harvester

Barn

Plough

Trailer

Tractor

Horse

Goat

Pony

Foal

Field

Trough

Donkey

Cow

Calf

Bull

Piglet

Pig

Sheep

Lamb

Corn

Butterflies

Caterpillar

Badger

Rabbits

Field mouse

Flowers

Grass

Fox

29

AT THE WILDLIFE PARK

There are a lot of wild animals. How many birds can you see? Which is the tallest animal? Can you find the cheetah? Which animal has a stripy tail?

Gorilla

Ostrich

Cheetah

Zebra

Giraffe

Crocodile

Lion

Bird

Antelope

Lioness

Lion cub

Chimpanzee

Hippopotamus

Rhinoceros

Leopard

Elephant

Flamingos

30

Owls

Grizzly bear

Wolf

Who is diving?

Penguin

Seal

Polar bear

Eagle

Toucan

Koala

Parrot

Lemur

Kangaroo

Who likes to eat bananas?

Kiwi

Panther

Snake

Tiger

Panda

Monkey

31

SPRING

Kite

Showers

Rainbow

Bees

Umbrella

Bird's nest

Blossom

Lambs

Daffodils

Tulips

Puddle

Ladybird

What's the weather like in spring?

It's rainy. It's windy. It's warm.

Do you need an umbrella in the spring?

SEASONS AND WEATHER

Sunshine

Butterflies

Thunder storm

Lightning

Camping

Sunglasses

Ice lolly

Sundress

Sunflowers

Holidays

Strawberries

What's the weather like in summer?

It's hot. It's humid. It's sticky.

What's your favourite thing to do in summer?

SUMMER

AUTUMN

Crow

Red leaves

Harvest

Apples

Hay bales

Halloween

Scarecrow

Yellow leaves

Pumpkins

Rake

What's the weather like in autumn?

It's foggy. It's chilly. It's damp.

What do you like most about autumn?

Snowflakes

Woolly hat

Sledge

Icicles

Winter coat

Bird feeder

Toboggan

Snowman

What's the weather like in winter?

It's frosty. It's cold. It's icy and freezing.

Snow shovel

Scarf

What special things do you do in the winter?

WINTER

Sea captain

Vet

Architect

Flight attendant

Make-up artist

Dustman

Shop assistant

Chef

Blogger

Movie star

Scientist

Juggler

Police officer

Zoo keeper

Butcher

Forklift driver

Accountant

34

JOBS PEOPLE DO

What will you do when you grow up? Would you like to be a movie star or a juggler? Do you dream of being a chef or a vet or a musician? What is your favourite job?

Acrobats

Waiter

Road worker

Hairdresser

Mechanic

35

Musician

Pilot

Miner

Film director

Soldier

Electrician

Porter

Fisherman

THINGS THAT GO

Aeroplane

Do you like cars and trucks and machines?
Which one would you use to go on holiday?
Which one would you choose to go to the moon?

Glider

Fighter jet

Rocket

Helicopter

Hot-air balloon

Aeroplane

Container ship

36

Hang glider

Drone

Cruise ship

Yacht

Fishing boat

Windsurfer

Sailing boat

speedboat

Submarine

Who is stuck in the tree?

Police car

Fire engine

Dump truck

Digger

Concrete mixer

Car

Motor scooter

Caravan

Minibus

Racing car

Tram

Scooter

Motorbike

Lorry

Van

Bus

Ambulance

Bicycle

Train

37

SPORTS

Do you play any sports? Do you like swimming? Can you ride a bicycle? Choose your five favourite sports.

Poles

Skiing

Snowboarding

Slopes

Soccer

Athletics

Player

Cycling

Net

Volleyball

Ice hockey

Sailing

Surfing

Mountaineering

Racquet

Handball

Punchbag

Tennis

American football

Boxing

38

Bat

Table tennis

Gymnastics

Why is the giraffe so good at basketball?

Basketball

Cricket

Rowing

Oars

Motor racing

33

Bat

Baseball

Ball

Rugby

Swimming

Horse riding

39

Saddle

Hockey stick

Hockey

Archery

Badminton

Golf

Rope

Skate boarding

Skating

Motorbike racing

1

Rock climbing

COLOURS AND SHAPES

What's your favourite colour? Is it green? Is it blue?
Do you know what all the shapes are called?

A red apple

Red

An orange carrot

Orange

A yellow banana

Yellow

A blue balloon

Blue

Purple

A purple t-shirt

Brown

A brown teddy

A gold cup

Gold

Black

A black cat

Pink

A pink rose

Green

A green cabbage

White

A white dog

A light blue bow

Light blue

Dark blue

A dark blue trainer

Grey

A grey mouse

Striped

A striped blouse

Chequered

A chequered shirt

Circle

Square

Rectangle

Triangle

Oval

Diamond

Star

Heart

Cross

Crescent

Arrow

Cone

Sphere

Cube

Hexagon

Pentagon

Octagon

Crown

40

CAN YOU SPOT?

Look at the jumble below.
Can you spot

1. A yellow heart?
2. A blue cube?
3. A red star?
4. A chequered balloon?
5. A striped hexagon?
6. A pink mouse?
7. A black & white cat?
8. A blue shirt?
9. A purple sphere?
10. A green arrow?

43

NUMBERS AND TIME

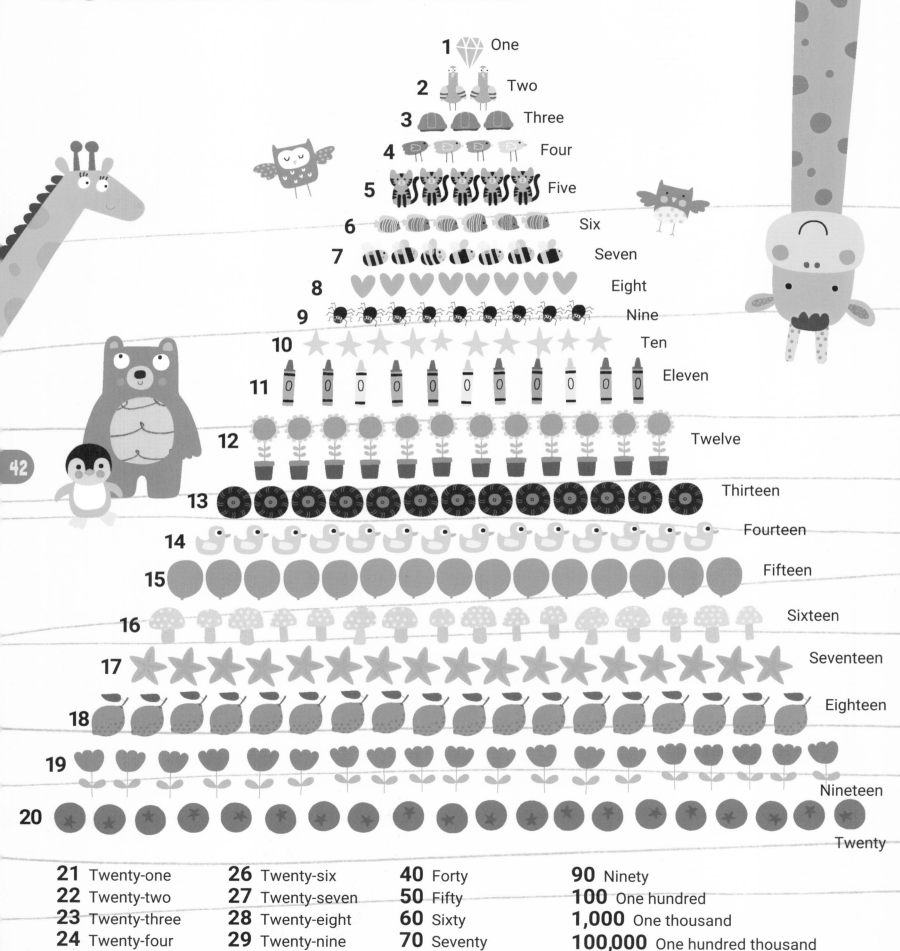

1 One
2 Two
3 Three
4 Four
5 Five
6 Six
7 Seven
8 Eight
9 Nine
10 Ten
11 Eleven
12 Twelve
13 Thirteen
14 Fourteen
15 Fifteen
16 Sixteen
17 Seventeen
18 Eighteen
19 Nineteen
20 Twenty

21 Twenty-one	26 Twenty-six	40 Forty	90 Ninety
22 Twenty-two	27 Twenty-seven	50 Fifty	100 One hundred
23 Twenty-three	28 Twenty-eight	60 Sixty	1,000 One thousand
24 Twenty-four	29 Twenty-nine	70 Seventy	100,000 One hundred thousand
25 Twenty-five	30 Thirty	80 Eighty	1,000,000 One million

42

Days of the week

Sunrise
MORNING

Sunshine
AFTERNOON

Sunset
EVENING

Dark

NIGHT

Calendar

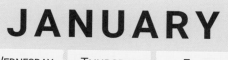

JANUARY

MONDAY	TUESDAY	WEDNESDAY	THURSDAY	FRIDAY	SATURDAY	SUNDAY
30	31	1	2	3	4	5
6	7	8	9	10	11	12
13	14	15	16	17	18	19
20	21	22	23	24	25	26
27	28	29	30	31	1	2

What day is it today? What month is it?

Months of the year

43

JANUARY	FEBRUARY	MARCH	APRIL
27	**4**	**18**	**30**
Monday	Tuesday	Wednesday	Thursday

What day is your birthday? How old will you be?

MAY	JUNE	JULY	AUGUST
8	**13**	**12**	**14**
Friday	Saturday	Sunday	Friday

What month do you go on holiday?

SEPTEMBER	OCTOBER	NOVEMBER	DECEMBER
30	**26**	**10**	**19**
Wednesday	Monday	Tuesday	Saturday

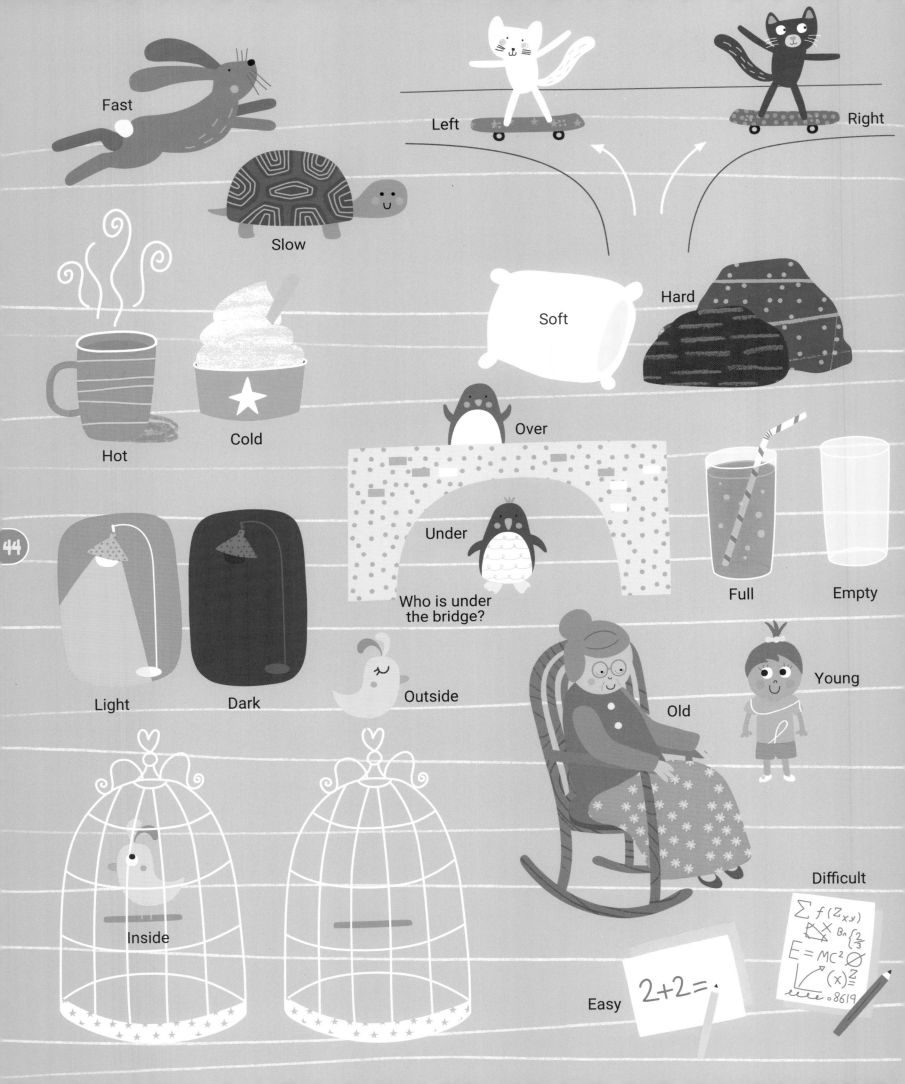

Fast

Slow

Left

Right

Soft

Hard

Hot

Cold

Over

Under

Who is under
the bridge?

Full

Empty

Light

Dark

Outside

Old

Young

Inside

Difficult

Easy

$2+2=$

$$\sum f(z_{xy})$$
$B_n \{ \frac{2}{3}$
$E = MC^2 \varnothing$
$\sqrt{(x)^2}$
.8619

44

OPPOSITES

Is it hot or cold today? Are you short or tall? Many words can be matched with others that mean exactly the opposite.

Alive

Back

Front

Fat

Thin

Clean

Short

Dirty

Closed

Dead

Long

Open

Old

New

Big

Small

RESTAURANT

Appetiser

Fish

Glass of wine

Wine bottle

Specials

Menu

Napkins

Soup

Steak

Diner

Gelato

Dessert

Waiter

Cashier

Tablecloth

Bill

Cash register

Credit card

Tray

Restaurant

Waitress

46

Food truck

Customer

Chips

Ice cream cart

Sandwich

Soft drink

Hamburger

Pizza

Hot dogs

Ketchup

Mustard

EATING OUT

Do you like to eat out? What's your favourite takeaway food? Do you like hamburgers and pizza? Yes? But you should eat some salad too!

Fried chicken

47

Tacos

Kebab

Vendor

Coffee machine

Salt & pepper

Curry

Food cart

FEELINGS

Do your feelings change a lot? Most people feel different things every day. They can be sad, scared or bored and then happy, excited or proud all on the same day!

Scared

Exhausted

Cheeky

Confused

Happy

Sad

Safe

48

Hopeful

Grumpy

Jealous

Proud

Sorry

Surprised

Relaxed

Angry

Tired

When you feel sad you should tell your Mum or Dad, or a teacher or friend.

Hot

Shy

Disappointed

Love

Bored

Nervous

Silly

Guilty

Ecstatic

Worried

Depressed

Frustrated

Cold

Disgusted

Sick

Smug

Lonely

Weepy

49

I can hide

I can slide

I can climb

I can skip

I can run

I can jump

I can throw

We can play

I can carry things

I can write

I can wave

I can catch

I can stand

We can wait

I can paint

I can read

I can drink

50

I can draw

I can sleep

I can crawl

I can sit

I can ride

We can talk

I can shout

I can leap

I can sweep

I can eat

We can dance

I can smile

I can hop

THINGS I CAN DO

There are so many things we know how to do!
Can you do them too? Which things do you
like doing best?

I can pull

I can push

I can cook

I can hear

I can chop

I can slice

I can walk

I can watch TV

51

TRAIN STATION

Have you visited a train station?
Have you ridden on a train?

Train driver

Train

Carriage

Engine

Platform

52

Ticket machine

Tourists

Arrivals

Kiosk

Luggage

Information desk

Escalator

Underground

AIRPORT

Have you been to the airport? Have you flown on a plane?

Control tower

Hangar

Mobile stairs

Terminal

Baggage truck

Private jet

Runway

Passenger jet

Duty free

5
1
2
3
8

Departures

Check in

Ticket desk

Café

1
2
5
8
3

Security guard

Arrivals

Metal detector

Passport

Baggage

Boarding card

Trolley

Passenger

The Sun
Slnko

Galaxy

Asteroids

Comet

Mercury

Venus

Earth

Mars

Spaceship

Space station

Telescope

Cosmonaut

Lander

UFO

Aliens

PlarPlanetnéta

54

SKYSCAPE

What can you see if you look up at the sky?
Can you see the sun, and the moon and some
stars? Can you see spaceships or aliens?

Star

Helmet

Moon

Equator

Spacesuit

Astronaut

Earth

Satellite

Meteorite

Constellation

55

Black hole

Falling star

Jupiter

Saturn

Uranus

Neptune

MUSEUM

Do you like paintings and statues? Do you like to see dinosaur bones? Go a museum!

Shield

costumes

Bust

Totem

Sword

Hammer

Masterpiece

Painting

Teddy bear

Puppets

Crown

Security officer

Suit of armour

Mastodon skeleton

Visitors

Jewel

Vase

Curator

Thief

Dinosaur skeleton

Pedestal

AQUARIUM

What animals stay in an aquarium?
Have you been to visit them?

Tropical fish

Sea turtle

Scallop

Stingray

Swordfish

Jellyfish

Whale

Octopus

Dolphin

Seahorses

Shark

Squid

Shrimp

Lobster

Seaweed

Angler fish

Coral

Visitors

57

Glass slipper

Carriage

Magic
wand

Monster

Prince

Cinderella

Fairy godmother

Good fairy

Broomstick

Witch

58

Toad

Castle

Princess

Wizard

Ogre

Palace

Unicorn

King

Queen

Ghost

STORY WORDS

Do you like stories? The ones that start "Once upon a time..." and end "...and they all lived happily ever after"? Can you spot some of your favourite characters?

Mermaid

Giant

Beautiful swan

Arrow

Bow

Ugly duckling

Skull and crossbones

Dragon

Knight

Eye patch

Sword

Treasure trove

Treasure

Pirate

Curse

Bad fairy

Sleeping beauty

INDEX

61

62